ANDRE AGASSI

D1039820

ANDRE AGASSI

Reaching the Top–Again

Jeff Savage

Lerner Publications Company • Minneapolis

To Lindsey Herdell, a future writing star

Information for this book was obtained from the following sources:
Associated Press, Chicago Tribune, Esquire, Forbes, McCall's, Newsweek, New York Times, People Weekly, San Francisco Chronicle, The Sporting News, Sports Illustrated, and *Time.*

This book is available in two bindings:
Library binding by Lerner Publications Company
Soft cover by First Avenue Editions
241 First Avenue North
Minneapolis, Minnesota 55401

International Standard Book Number: 0-8225-2894-0 (lib. bdg.)
International Standard Book Number: 0-8225-9750-0 (pbk.)

LIBRARY OF CONGRESS CATALOGING-IN-PUBLICATION DATA

Savage, Jeff, 1961–
    Andre Agassi : reaching the top, again / Jeff Savage.
      p.   cm.
    Includes index.
    Summary: A biography of the talented and colorful tennis player who won the Wimbledon championship in 1992 and earned the number one ranking in 1995.
    ISBN 0-8225-2894-0 (hardcover : alk. paper)
    ISBN 0-8225-9750-0 (pbk.)
    1. Agassi, Andre, 1970–   — Juvenile literature. 2. Tennis players — United States — Biography — Juvenile literature.
    [1. Agassi, Andre, 1970–   . 2. Tennis players.] I. Title.
GV994.A43S38   1997
796.342'092
[B] — dc21   96–48970

Manufactured in the United States of America
1 2 3 4 5 6 – JR – 02 01 00 99 98 97

Contents

A Golden Moment

"Aaannndreee!!!" cried the voices of young girls in the crowd. Andre Agassi tried not to listen. He stood on the olive green tennis court at Stone Mountain and fingered the strings of his racket. "Aaannndreee!!!" they cried.

It is hard not to hear the squeals of teens calling out your name, even if you are in the middle of the biggest tennis match of your life. Andre smiled and looked up. His face was warm and buttery. His brown eyes twinkled and a thousand hearts went atwitter.

Andre is the sweetheart of men's tennis. Anywhere he goes, a teenybopper brigade is there to greet him with puppy love. But Andre is also a tennis master. He is a human backboard against serves and a steady server himself. He is also a shot-making genius with his double-fisted backhand and laser forehand. He hits blistering ground strokes by snapping his wrist, as if he were flicking a flyswatter. And on this warm summer afternoon in 1996, as the Georgia sun played hide-and-seek with the clouds, Andre was on the verge of winning the biggest prize he could ever imagine—an Olympic gold medal.

Across the net from Andre was a swift opponent from Spain named Sergi Bruguera. From the start, Bruguera never had a chance. Andre peppered shots at him from all angles, and the speedy Spaniard wasn't able to keep up. "The way I'm playing today," Andre said later, "it didn't matter who was on the other side of the net." After Andre steamrollered Bruguera in the first set, six games to two, a reporter from Spain knew his countryman was doomed. The reporter gathered his pen and notepad and left the press box, muttering, "Bruguera is only interested in silver. He will lose within an hour." The reporter was right. Andre won the second set, 6–3, and took a commanding 5–1 lead in the third, as chants of "U-S-A, U-S-A" rang out in the stadium.

Andre's family and friends at courtside waved and cheered. They jumped up and down with the rest of the crowd. One of these happy fans was Brooke Shields, the glamorous actress and model who was engaged to be married to Andre. Next to Brooke, with a big grin on his face, was Andre's father, Mike Agassi. Mike rarely attends Andre's matches because they make him nervous. But he was so proud that

Andre had reached the final that he surprised his son the night before by flying in from Las Vegas. Mike knew what his son was up against. It wasn't just Sergi Bruguera of Spain. It was history. No American had won an Olympic gold in men's tennis in 72 years.

Brooke Shields and Andre have found their friendship helps them with the pressures of being famous.

Seventy-two years. The last U.S. gold medalist was Vincent Richards in 1924. Could Andre beat the odds? His father had come to find out. Winning a medal held personal meaning for Mike, too. He had competed in the Olympics twice himself, in boxing, for Iran in 1948 and 1952. He did not win a gold medal. Maybe his son would.

With Bruguera serving, Andre smacked a forehand return to the corner for a point. Then he sliced a backhand that clipped the baseline for a second winner. Finally he whistled another forehand past Bruguera to take a 40–0 lead.

Brad Gilbert once played professional tennis. He became Andre's coach in 1994.

Andre needed one more point to win the gold medal. But Bruguera did not quit. He fought back to win the next two points.

Andre stood at the baseline and nervously wiped his hands on his baggy blue denim shorts. He twisted the Swiss Army watch on his wrist. He tugged at his cap. He jiggled one of the zippers on his sweat-soaked bicycle shirt. Tennis players traditionally wear white, but Andre has always been a rebel. "If you stuck me in white clothing," he once said, "I'd go flip burgers for a living." Andre admits he is sensitive about his looks. He lives by the motto: *Image is everything.* That is why he had cut off his rock-and-roll hair a year earlier at Brooke's apartment in New York. His hair, long and flowing and the color of cream soda, had been part of his identity since he'd been a teenager. But his hairline was receding, and that embarrassed him. So he cut off his hair and started a new image—the bald Andre. He didn't change completely, however. He kept his flashy wardrobe. And, of course, he kept his jewelry box filled with earrings.

Andre's earrings on this day were gold hoops that matched the color of the first-place medal. They dangled in the blazing sunshine, giving his face a bit of a sparkle as he swayed from side to side. He crouched low, awaiting Brugeura's serve. *One more point,* he thought to himself. *One more point.*

Bruguera's serve came in. Andre was ready for it. He planted his feet, coiled his body, and drove forward through the ball, ripping a forehand that Bruguera had no chance to play. The ball skidded past Bruguera's feet for a clean winner, and the stadium crowd erupted. Andre pumped his fists mightily. Then he doffed his cap and blew kisses all around. As the crowd yelled for him, Andre threw his arms out toward his family. Brooke came bounding out of the stands onto the court, followed by his father and then his brother, Phillip. Andre's coach, Brad Gilbert, and his best friend, Perry Rogers, came too. They all hugged amid cries of "U-S-A, U-S-A."

The world's four greatest tennis tournaments are the Australian Open, the French Open, Wimbledon, and the U.S. Open. These four are called Grand Slam tournaments. Every player wants to win a Grand Slam. Andre had already won *three* Slams. Yet in the press tent after the Olympic final, Andre ranked his gold-medal victory ahead of them all. "This is the greatest accomplishment I've ever had in this sport," Andre told reporters. "To me, this is quite amazing."

Moments later, he changed into a warmup outfit and returned to the stadium court to receive his medal. He was delighted to see that the crowd had remained for the ceremony. He took his place on the top platform of the victory stand and an Olympic official appeared before him, holding the gold medal.

Andre, wearing his gold medal, stands between silver medalist Sergi Bruguera, left, and bronze medal-winner Leander Paes during the 1996 Olympic ceremony.

Andre leaned forward to allow the medal to be draped around his neck. The American flag was raised as the national anthem was played. Andre thought of his father and smiled. And then two tears rolled down his cheek.

Andre's long hair set him apart from other tennis players.

14

Prisoner of the Court

Andre was born in Las Vegas, Nevada, on April 29, 1970, only a few miles from where he still lives. He is the youngest of the four children of Emmanuel (Mike) and Elizabeth (Betty) Agassi. It was his father, Mike, who molded Andre into a tennis player.

Mike Agassi grew up in Iran at an American mission church. As a boy, he got a job watering and tending two tennis courts behind the church. He was fascinated by watching the American soldiers play tennis. In 1952, Mike immigrated to Chicago, Illinois, where he took a job waiting tables at a hotel. He didn't know much English, but he did know how to box. He had boxed on Iran's Olympic team, and he dreamed of one day becoming a world champion. He was ready to turn professional one night at New York's Madison Square Garden in 1955, but the boxer he was supposed to fight backed out. Mike was matched up with another opponent, a more powerful boxer with 30 professional wins. Mike was sure to lose, but he was told it would be good for his career. As Mike was about to enter the ring, he stopped and went back to the locker room. He crawled out a window to the street and took a train back to Chicago. The next day he bought a tennis racket.

Mike became obsessed with tennis. He made up his mind that his children would become champion tennis players at any cost. He moved his family west where tennis could be played outdoors all year. Unable to find work in California, the Agassi family settled in Las Vegas, where Betty found a job at an employment agency. Mike worked at night as a waiter at a casino. He taught tennis to his children during the day.

Each school day was the same. The four children—Rita, Phil, Tami, and Andre—would rise at 6 o'clock in the morning for an hour of tennis practice before school. They would practice three hours more after school, eat dinner, do their homework, and go to bed. Weekends were devoted almost entirely to tennis. They practiced on an outdoor court at the Tropicana Hotel. Mike sometimes had eight ball machines going at once, shooting ball after ball for his children to hit back. Rita, Phil, and Tami each hit 7,000 balls a week. Andre hit twice that. "Andre had the desire," Mike says. "I don't know if the desire was just to please his parents, but he had it."

Tennis was all Andre knew. When Andre was an infant, Mike hung a tennis ball over Andre's crib to focus his eyes. When Andre could sit in a high chair and hold a spoon, his father put a Ping-Pong paddle in Andre's hand and strung up a balloon for him to try to hit. When Andre was learning to walk, Mike stuck a full-sized racket in his fist and allowed him to swing at objects around the house. Betty had to take everything off the kitchen counters after Andre whacked a salt shaker through a glass door. When Andre was two and a half years old, his father taped a racket to his hand and put him on the tennis court. Six months later, Andre could rally with his father. "Dad raised me to play," Andre says. "As a kid, all you know is what you see around you, and tennis was all I saw. I never considered doing anything else."

Since Mike worked for a casino, he was able to persuade pros who came to town for tournaments to rally a few minutes with Andre. One of Andre's earliest memories is of a small crowd encircling the Tropicana court as he hit with legendary player Bobby Riggs. "I remember being watched," Andre says, "and I remember liking it." On his fourth birthday, Andre rallied with Jimmy Connors. He also hit with other greats like Bjorn Borg. "Meet my little champion," is how his father would introduce young Andre to people.

When Andre was five, his family moved to a house where Mike could build a tennis court out back. Mike saved $860 to buy a ball machine, which meant lots of hitting for Andre. Las Vegas is located in a desert where it hardly ever rains, but Andre enjoyed the rare times it did. Rain meant no tennis.

At six, Andre signed his first autograph, after hitting with professional player Ilie Nastase. At seven, he began playing in tournaments. He won his first nine matches. Every other weekend, Mike and Betty would load the kids in the station wagon and drive to Southern California, about 300 miles away, so the children could compete in junior tournaments. They would stay together in one room at a motel and discuss strategy at night.

At the tournaments, Mike developed a reputation as a loudmouth and a complainer. For Mike, it was win or else. Jim Courier, another tennis superstar, remembers the first time he saw Andre. It was at a 12-and-under tournament in San Diego, and Andre had just taken third place. Courier watched as Andre left the court with his father. He saw Mike fling Andre's third-place trophy in a garbage can.

Andre's father figured that if his children hated losing enough, they wouldn't lose. He yelled at them in public if they lost and sometimes even if they won. The pressure was intense. One time Rita came off the court after losing a match in a national tournament and vomited blood. By the age of 13, she had bleeding ulcers from stress.

When Andre was 13, his father saw a segment on the television show *60 Minutes* about a special tennis school for youngsters, the Nick Bollettieri Tennis Academy in Bradenton, Florida. Mike asked a local tennis official if he thought it would be a good place for Andre to master his skills. "It's an Army camp," the official told him. "But the kid will make it because of you." Andre was pulled out of school midway through eighth grade and sent across the continent to Florida.

Andre's parents, Mike and Betty Agassi, and his brother, Phillip, helped Andre become a tremendous tennis player.

A part of Andre was afraid to leave home. He feared the academy and its reputation for strict rules. But another part of him wanted to go. He was eager to become a professional tennis player. He knew his best chance would be to learn at the academy.

Andre found that nearly 200 junior tennis players from all over the world attended the academy. They lived in dormitory rooms and ate their meals in a big cafeteria. They attended school in the morning and were on the courts by one o'clock, learning tennis.

Nick Bollettieri, the camp director, liked Andre from the start. "I relate well to Andre," Bollettieri explained. "He's a character and I'm a character. He's my friend."

The cost of the academy was $20,000 a year. Andre's father wasn't sure how long he could afford to keep his son there. But Bollettieri was so impressed with Andre's basic tennis ability that he gave him a full scholarship. Andre's father would not have to pay anything.

Andre was used to winning, but at camp he began losing his share of matches. He threw rackets and temper tantrums. Each morning for school, he dressed in black to reflect his mood. He was angry and miserable. "He was never much of a student," remembered Courier, his roommate at the academy. "He was always getting in trouble. He was a bit of a punk."

Andre smashed rackets into the ground, kicked them over the net, and threw them into the pool. He went through 40 Prince rackets a year. In one pathetic match, he smashed seven rackets.

"It was tough on him," said Perry Rogers, "A young kid like that, so far away." Andre called Rogers long-distance often, and the two friends talked for hours. One time, Andre even sold his tennis gear to buy Rogers a plane ticket to come visit him. "He saw me in Vegas, having fun," said Rogers. "And here he was, missing everything, not growing, *losing*. He was nearly crying on the phone once. 'What am I doing this for?' he said. He was scared. He was scared he was going through all this to be a tennis player for nothing. He was scared he wasn't going to make it."

But Andre worked hard at his tennis game. He learned new techniques and perfected the specialty of his ground strokes—hitting the ball on the rise. He became one of Bollettieri's favorites, which bothered other students. Monica Seles trained at the academy but her parents became so upset with the amount of time Bollettieri spent with Andre that they pulled her out and moved away. Despite the special treatment, Andre was not happy. "I hated it there," he said. "I hated growing up in Florida, 3,000 miles away from home. But the only way I could get out of that academy was to succeed. So that became my inspiration: to do well so that I could escape."

Phillip Agassi, Andre's big brother, helped him get used to playing on the professional tennis tour.

Teenage Professional

On May 1, 1986, two days after his 16th birthday, Andre "escaped." He didn't leave the Bollettieri academy, but he became a professional. As a professional, he could play in pro tournaments and keep any prize money he won. He could see if all the years of hitting tennis balls meant something. He could pursue his dream of being a tennis star.

Bollettieri helped Andre get his first pro contract, a $25,000 deal from Nike. In return, Andre would wear Nike sneakers in tournaments. He immediately began playing in tournaments around the country and sometimes overseas. His older brother, Phil, traveled everywhere with him, sleeping on the floor of his motel room. Phil worked as Andre's manager, arranging for flights and rental cars, planning meals, and making sure Andre's tennis equipment was in proper condition.

Andre didn't win any tournaments his first year, but he played well enough to be ranked 91st in the world. It was not his performance, however, that earned him a reputation—it was his personality. Andre acted wild and crazy. He became known as "the bad boy of tennis." At the Nevada Open, he angrily pounded balls into the fence, made crude gestures with his racket, and yelled, "Shut up," when the crowd applauded his opponent. At a match in Florida, he showed up wearing jeans, lipstick, eyeliner, and earrings. Before another tournament, he shaved his head. At another, he got a mohawk haircut and dyed the mohawk blond. Tournament pressure made Andre anxious and moody. Bollettieri, his coach, was so furious about Andre's behavior that he criticized Andre in front of other players. Andre threatened to leave the academy. "You people don't realize how tough it is on kids," Andre told his coach. Bollettieri began to understand the pressure Andre was feeling.

As Andre's skills improved, he started winning more matches. Early in 1987, he beat his first three opponents at the Stratton Tennis Tournament in Vermont to reach the semifinals against four-time U.S. Open champion John McEnroe. Though Andre lost the match, he won McEnroe's respect. "No one's ever hit the ball that hard against me," McEnroe said. "He's still a kid, but he has the confidence and the attitude of a champion."

Nick Bollettieri runs a tennis camp for players who want to become professionals. Andre developed his tennis skills with Bollettieri's instruction.

Sometimes the pressure got to be too much for Andre to handle. When he lost in the first round of a tournament in Washington, D.C., he left the court in tears, yelling that he was quitting tennis. He ran to a nearby park and gave his rackets to two old men sitting on a park bench playing checkers.

In the winter of 1987, Andre met Fritz Glauss, the pro tour's traveling minister. Andre began reading the Bible every day. He got together often with another teenage star, Michael Chang, for Bible readings. Soon he became a Christian. "There are only two directions in life," Andre says. "One that leads to helping others and one that leads to selfish purposes. I wasn't on my way to helping others. I was facing a lot of questions in my life. I knew there had to be more important things than tennis, money, and fame."

With religion as his calming influence, Andre became even better at tennis. He beat Jimmy Connors, the star he had rallied with on his fourth birthday, at a tournament in Amelia Island, Florida. Then at a tournament in Brazil, Andre earned his first Tour title and a first-place check for $90,000. He still had his zest for clowning around. Once he sent chicken wings by Federal Express to his pal Perry Rogers, who was attending college at Georgetown University. But Andre wasn't mature enough yet to do well in the big tournaments, the Grand Slams. He lost in the second round of the French Open and in the first rounds of Wimbledon and the U.S. Open.

Tennis has had certain unwritten codes of conduct since its beginning in France in the fourteenth century. One such code is that players dress in white. Andre laughed at that tradition. He started wearing wild outfits like colorful pink bicycle tights and black shorts, jazzy purple-on-black shirts, and red shoes. His Day-Glo look offended tennis officials, but there was little they could do. Except for Wimbledon, no tournament had official, written rules of dress. Besides, most fans enjoyed this new teen star and his radical look. "I do everything by extremes," Andre said. That attitude wooed legions of fans. Andre began applauding opponents' shots, tossing sweat-soaked shirts and extra pairs of denim shorts to spectators, blowing kisses to the crowd. He was hamming it up.

Andre's wild outfits caused a stir at tournaments.

And then, like a flash of heat lightning from the Nevada desert, Andre became a star. In 1988, he won six tennis titles. Mats Wilander, the top-ranked player in the world, also won six that year. No other player won more.

Kids have always been Andre's favorite fans.

At the French Open, where Andre argued daily with tournament officials about his wild outfits, he blew away five opponents to reach the semifinals. He did this despite eating every night for two weeks at McDonald's. "He thinks that's why he did so well," said tennis star Pete Sampras. Andre was interviewed by more journalists than any other player. Girls threw flowers to him on the court and screamed for his autograph. In his semifinal match, Andre lost to Wilander, the No. 1 player, in five sets, and Wilander went on to win the title. But when tennis fans remember the 1988 tournament on the red clay of Stade Roland Garros, they remember the hysteria over new teen idol Andre Agassi.

Andre was like a Hollywood celebrity in the tennis world. His sister Rita started the Andre Agassi Fan Club. Soon Andre was receiving 2,000 letters a week. He was a breath of fresh air for tennis, which hadn't had an American phenom like this since Jimmy Connors burst onto the scene in 1974.

Andre won six tournaments and $822,062 in 1988. At the end of the year, he was ranked No. 3 in the world. Mike Agassi's plan to make his son a tennis star had worked. Andre was so popular that Donnay Company offered him a five-year deal. The company paid him $6 million to use its rackets.

When some athletes and entertainers hit the big time as Andre did, they lose interest in their old friends and start moving with a faster crowd. But Andre didn't change. He didn't get a big ego. He still enjoyed the simple life. To celebrate New Year's Eve, he packed up a stack of pizzas, several six-packs of diet soda, a tent, and four sleeping bags. He and his girlfriend, Amy Moss, drove with another couple from Las Vegas to Malibu, California, in his mother's Range Rover. They spent the evening on the beach, ringing in the New Year by watching the waves roll in. They celebrated the year gone by and cheered Andre for his achievements. They talked of what the future might hold. Whatever else was in store, Andre hoped the future held something special for him: a Grand Slam title.

At the 1989 U.S. Open, Andre advanced to the semifinals.

Not Quite Good Enough

The Davis Cup is an international men's team championship that began in 1900. The United States hadn't won the Cup in six years when 1989 U.S. captain Tom Gorman turned to a fresh new face—Andre Agassi. It is an honor to be chosen for the Davis Cup team and Andre proudly accepted the challenge. He replaced John McEnroe as the team's No. 1 singles player. Even McEnroe told Andre it was a wise change. "He told me I'm the next guy who can do it for America," Andre said.

In Andre's first match, he beat Jaime Yzaga to lead the United States to a 3–0 victory in Lima, Peru. Two months later, on the bronze dirt courts of Buenos Aires, the U.S. team faced Argentina. With an icy wind blowing tiles off the stadium roof, Andre warmed up with a few forehands, backhands, and serves. Then he crushed Argentina's Martin Jaite 6–2,

6–2, 6–1. "Amazing," coach Gorman said. But Andre showed his youth as well. Leading 4–0 in the third set, but with Jaite serving with a 40–0 lead, Andre decided to just let his opponent win the game. Andre turned to his personal coach, Nick Bollettieri, who was watching from the stands. "Watch this," said Andre. Then he reached out and caught Jaite's serve, giving Jaite the game. Andre thought the crowd would enjoy his showboating. Instead, they booed him for embarrassing their player. Even McEnroe was surprised at Andre's poor judgment. "Andre is young and naive, but that was unbelievable," Mac said. "Too much ham, too insulting to the other guy. Hopefully, he learned a lesson."

The United States defeated Argentina but lost in the next round of the Davis Cup competition. So Andre turned his attention to the Grand Slams. At the French Open, he reached the third round, only to lose to Courier, his former roommate at Bollettieri's academy. Andre skipped Wimbledon because he did not want to have to wear white clothing. At the U.S. Open in Flushing Meadow, New York, he was just two victories away from winning a Grand Slam tournament, but his hopes were dashed in a semifinal loss to Ivan Lendl. The loss was a disappointing end to a difficult year in which Andre won just one tournament. "I got really drained at the end of the year because I had played so much tennis," Andre admitted.

Jim Courier defeated Andre at the 1989 French Open.

"There was a lot of pressure, plus the expectations of people and expectations I put on myself. I had a lot of growing up to do. I still do."

By early 1990, Andre had solved two problems that had plagued him the previous year. He had improved his physical condition by hiring fitness coach Gil Reyes, the strength and conditioning coach at the University of Nevada at Las Vegas. Reyes put Andre through a strenuous daily workout that included jogging, sprinting, and a great amount of weight lifting. Andre also resolved a racket problem that started when he first began using Donnay models. "The racket twisted in his hand," said Bollettieri. Andre's father traveled to Belgium to work with the Donnay designers. Andre even used a Prince racket disguised as a Donnay by removing the Prince logos and stenciling a D on the strings.

Seeing double? Andre's on the right. His Donnay racket advertising double is on the left.

Finally, though, a racket was made that felt just right. Donnay executives rewarded Andre's patience by offering him a $20 million contract to use their company's rackets. Andre happily accepted.

Andre opened the year by winning a tournament in San Francisco and another in Key Biscayne, Florida. He went to Paris for the French Open, focused on winning. "Last year I had a plane reservation after every match," he said. "This year I packed two weeks' worth of socks." Andre rolled through his first four opponents as expected, then found himself across the net from defending champion Michael Chang in the quarterfinals. The clay surface at Roland Garros slows down the ball, which gives speedsters like Chang time to chase down most shots. But Andre blistered his ground strokes to whip Chang 6–1, 6–2, 4–6, 6–2. Then in the semifinals, Andre blasted past young Swedish star Jonas Svennson in four sets. He was one win away from his dream of a Grand Slam title.

Andres Gomez, Andre's opponent in the final, was a 30-year-old from Ecuador. Gomez held the mental edge of experience, but he would surely tire as the match went along. Gomez knew he had to get to Andre early. And he did. He sizzled an ace past Andre to win the first set, 6–3. Andre rallied to win the second set, 6–2. But Gomez won the next two sets, 6–4, 6–4, to deny Andre his first Slam. "He was going for every shot," Andre said, "and it worked."

Andre was the most popular player in the world when he arrived at the U.S. Open that September. He had just made his first commercial for Canon cameras in which he was shown pounding balls in a frenzy and uttering the phrase that defined him: "Image is everything." In a stirring semifinal match against Boris Becker, with patches of blue sky overhead, Andre delighted the crowd with breathtaking shots that skidded on the lines. After dropping the first set in a **tiebreaker,** he blitzed Becker 6–3, 6–2, 6–3 to reach his second Slam final.

Andre's opponent in the final would be Pete Sampras, another up-and-coming American. Sampras had watched Andre's match from the stands. "Becker had a bad game plan against Andre," Sampras said. "He tried to outslug Andre. He should have come to the net as soon as possible." In the final, Sampras did just that. He overwhelmed Andre with a superb **serve-and-volley** game to win in straight sets. "Why are you so slow?" Andre yelled at himself several times during the match. The loss seemed to break Andre's spirit.

Andre was frustrated that he could not win a Grand Slam event. He told his brother to go home. He put down his racket. "I didn't want to play," Andre said, "because I felt I had compromised so much of my life to get where I was." He began lifting weights every day for hours at a time.

Enthusiastic Andre electrified the 1990 U.S. Open crowd.

The rivalry between Andre and Pete Sampras has been one of the top matchups in the 1990s.

Andre went to the Tour World Championship only because the eight highest-ranked men were invited and he was No. 4. Andre whipped Sampras in the first round, beat Becker in the semifinals, and routed Stefan Edberg in the final.

Andre's confidence that he would one day win a Grand Slam was already shaky. At the 1991 French Open, it shattered into a million pieces. As usual, Andre cruised through the early rounds. In the semifinals, he returned the mighty serves of Boris Becker with ease, and he knocked out the star from Germany in four sets. "As a player, he is in a different league," Becker said afterward. "Andre is ready to win a Slam. But he must keep his nerve."

On a dreary June afternoon in Paris two days later, Andre stepped onto the red clay court with a face of intense concentration. There would be no hamming it up, no throwing sweaty shirts to the fans, no prancing around on this day. He was going to play great tennis and win a Grand Slam title.

His opponent was archrival Jim Courier. Andre came out blazing. He crushed Courier in the first set 6–3. He led 3–1 in the second set and he was on his way. Then it started to rain. The match was halted.

Coaches are not allowed to discuss strategy with players during the match, but since a tarp covered the court, Courier's coach could meet with him. The coach told Courier to stand 10 feet behind the baseline on Andre's serves and then rush to the net. The rain stopped, play resumed, and Courier's new strategy worked. He rallied to win the second set, dropped the third, then won the last two sets to beat Andre.

Andre felt as though someone had sneaked up from behind and knocked him off his feet. If only it hadn't rained. If only Courier hadn't talked with his coach. If only Andre hadn't lost his momentum. In the media room afterward, Andre was quiet and sullen. "The pessimistic side of me questions if I'll ever win [a Grand Slam tournament]," he whispered. And then he stood up and walked out. It was a wrenching defeat and it would bother Andre for nearly a year.

Ready to Be the Best

No, Andre did not have a Grand Slam trophy, but he did have plenty of money. And he had a desire to buy cars. Not just for himself, but for almost everyone he knew or to whom he was related. Since signing his first big contract with Donnay two years earlier, Andre had bought 25 cars. He owned a Lamborghini, a Ferrari, several Cadillacs, white and black Porsches he named Bridget and Samantha, a sleek red Viper, a big Suburban, and an all-terrain Humvee. He bought a Cadillac for his father and a BMW for Perry Rogers when Rogers graduated from Georgetown. He even bought a red Eagle Talon sports car for his fitness trainer Gil Reyes's daughter on her 16th birthday.

Andre did not desert his old friends, but he found time to make new ones. He met legendary singer Barbra Streisand in New York, and they developed a close friendship. He made a rock-and-roll video with the Red Hot Chili Peppers. He had become wildly popular as a celebrity, not just as a tennis player.

Andre was living the good life and he was becoming lazy. He ate Big Macs for breakfast, candy for lunch, and pizza for dinner. In six months he gained 25 pounds. "I'm just a spoiled American who likes my baseball and my Taco Bell," he admitted.

Andre wanted to win a Grand Slam title so badly that he went to Wimbledon. It was his first time in London in four years. He told the regal All England Club officials that he had left his colorful skate-boarder outfits at home. He was prepared to dress all in white and the Wimbledon officials welcomed him with open arms. But with his chunky body slowing him down, Andre struggled through his first four matches. He was eliminated in the quarterfinals. Disappointed in himself, Andre returned to Las Vegas that night to assume his grunge look.

At the U.S. Open two months later, Andre was back in comfortable clothing, but he was still overweight. Aaron Krickstein blew him out in three pitiful sets. The press wrote that Andre was "heavy, slow, out of focus, off-target." Andre was embarrassed and hurt. When his father offered suggestions, Andre snapped, "Why should I listen to you?" He moved away from his parents to a home of his own.

Andre searched for answers. He tried different

rackets. He changed his serve, then changed back again. He hired a coach to help him with his volleys, then fired him a month later. He tried a low-fat diet but quit it after three weeks when he cramped up in a match. After Andre boarded a plane for France with his U.S. Davis Cup teammates, a flight attendant served him cheeseburgers. Andre had called ahead to order the special meal. When teammate Pete Sampras asked him about it, Andre insisted the cheeseburgers contained "your four basic food groups." In France, he ate mostly candy. "Big bags of Reese's and Snickers," according to Sampras.

Andre lost in the first round at the Milan Indoor Championship in Italy. He lost in the second round in tournaments in Arizona, Florida, Belgium, and Spain. He fell out of the top 10 in the world rankings for the first time in four years. "I think I need to come to terms with what makes me tick," he decided. "I go through stages where it seems no one can beat me, and then I go through stages where it seems any-one can beat me."

Then, all at once, Andre turned it around again. He was tired of losing, tired of feeling lousy, tired of being tired. He rededicated himself to tennis and trained hard. He gave up his beloved Big Gulps and Quarter Pounders and Junior Mints and lost some weight. He went to Paris for the French Open, where he had lost in the rain to Jim Courier a year earlier.

"It felt so unfair," Andre said of that defeat. "It made me doubt, it hurt my confidence, it made me second-guess myself. And it wasn't until last week that I said, 'I'm done with that.' " Andre blitzed through the first three rounds of the Open, then hammered Sampras in the quarterfinals. His out-of-shape body could only take him so far, though, and he lost in the semifinals. A month later, he went to Wimbledon.

A fortnight is two weeks, and that is how long Wimbledon lasts. On the 14th day of the tournament, Andre was still playing. He had fought his way past six opponents to reach the title match. In the quarterfinals, he beat three-time Wimbledon champion Boris Becker. "He hit shots that weren't in the book," Becker said. "You cannot play better tennis than Andre did." In the semifinals, he beat John McEnroe, another three-time champion, and he beat him in **straight sets.** "He was incredible," said McEnroe.

In the final match, Andre stood on the green shadow-striped grass of Centre Court, locked in a bitter struggle with a lanky and skilled opponent named Goran Ivanisevic. Each man had won two sets. Each had won three games in the fifth and final set. The first to win six games would be the champion of the greatest tournament in the world.

Ivanisevic had the most powerful serve on the planet, and he knew it. He described his game this way: "Serve, serve, serve. Forty aces. Win. Boring."

Andre's Wimbledon victory was his first Grand Slam title.

True to form, Ivanisevic had been ripping ace after ace past Andre—11 in the first set, 10 in the fifth, 37 for the day. Ivanisevic is a Croat whose country, the former Yugoslavia, at that moment was being torn apart by a bloody civil war. Ivanisevic might have been the crowd's favorite this day. But Andre's spell-binding charm made the fans of England forget all about Ivanisevic.

Fans love Andre's aggressive way of playing.

In the seventh game of the deciding set of the final, Andre found himself down a **break point.** He could have folded. Many in the crowd secretly feared he might. After all, he had reached three Grand Slam finals and lost them all. But Andre did not fail. He rushed to the net and hit a winning volley on the run. Then he served an ace. He eventually **held serve** to win the game and take the lead, four games to three.

Ivanisevic responded. He bombed Andre with titanic serves to win the eighth game and tie the score at four games apiece. Andre came back. He held serve to win the ninth game and the crowd roared. Now he led, five games to four. If he could somehow win against Ivanisevic's serve, just once, he could win a Grand Slam. "And this isn't just any Grand Slam," Andre said later, "it's *Wimbledon!*"

Ivanisevic stepped up to serve the 10th game. Trailing five games to four, he was suddenly struck by the pressure. He hit two bad serves for a **double fault.** He double-faulted again, and the score was 0–30. Ivanisevic pulled himself together to win the next two points, making it 30–30. But on the next point, he rushed to the net, and Andre whacked a forehand **passing shot** that grazed inside the line for a winner. For Andre, victory was one point away.

"I was scared, nervous, intimidated, and excited all at the same time," said Andre. It was match point. Ivanisevic smacked his first serve into the net. "My eyes lit up," said Andre. Ivanisevic's second serve was good. Andre ripped a backhand return right back at him. Ivanisevic chunked his backhand volley into the net. Andre collapsed in utter joy. "The next thing I look, nothing, except see guy down on floor," said Ivanisevic. "Oh, no. I lose Wimbledon. Unbelievable."

Unbelievable, yet true. Andre wept facedown in the grass until Ivanisevic stepped over the net and helped him up. They hugged and soon Andre was parading around Centre Court, holding aloft the golden Wimbledon trophy. Then, just as he had bowed to the dignitaries in the royal box on the way in, he bowed on the way out. He left the stadium with tears running down his face.

"This is the greatest title in the world," Andre told reporters. "It is the greatest achievement I have ever made." He returned to Las Vegas with the great trophy and proudly showed it to his father, who had watched the match on television. Mike was not as thrilled as Andre had hoped. "He told me how I lost the fourth set," Andre said.

At the U.S. Open in New York, there were Andre Agassi T-shirts, Andre Agassi hats, Andre Agassi pins, even Andre Agassi bumper stickers for sale. Barbra Streisand cheered for him from the stands as Andre beat his first three opponents. With his ponytail hanging from underneath his purple hat, Andre lost in the quarterfinals to his rival Jim Courier.

Goran Ivanisevic congratulates Andre at Wimbledon.

Everyone at Wimbledon could see how delighted Andre was with his first-place trophy.

Despite the loss, Andre was not discouraged. "I'm here for another 10 years," he said.

Andre capped the year by leading the U.S. team to victories over Sweden and Switzerland to win the Davis Cup title. How did he celebrate? By buying an airplane. Andre bought a 10-seat Lockheed JetStar for $2 million from Bruce McNall, owner of the Los Angeles Kings hockey team. Andre had the tail of the jet emblazoned with a large A and a flaming tennis ball. Then he stocked the galley with his favorite candy.

But just when Andre was flying high again, he suffered another fall. His right wrist had been bothering him more and more. By the time the 1993 tour season arrived, he was in sheer pain. A doctor's exam showed that Andre had tendinitis, the painful wear and tear of the tissue that connects muscle with bone. Surgery was recommended. Andre said no. He was afraid. But swinging a racket hurt so much that he lost interest in tennis once again. He stopped training and slept a lot. He got fat on McNuggets and Big Gulps. He canceled plans to play in his first Australian Open. Four months later, he skipped the French Open, too.

Andre insisted on playing Wimbledon in July. As the defending champion, he felt he had to be there. He took a series of cortisone injections to temporarily numb his wrist, then wrapped it in a blue brace. He showed up in London with a big belly and a double chin. Andre had played just one hour of tennis in the previous month. He hadn't played in a tournament since March. His wrist hurt so badly before the cortisone shots that he couldn't do a single push-up. "It's an honor to be here to defend the title," Andre said. "It's a privilege to be in this position."

Andre won his first three matches, then stunned everyone, including himself, when he beat Richard Krajicek in the fourth round in straight sets. "It's absolutely incredible," he said, "and I don't plan on stopping." But Pete Sampras edged him in the quarterfinals. "I gave it my best shot," Andre said.

Andre returned to Las Vegas where, a few days later, he received a letter in the mail from Nick Bollettieri. Bollettieri wrote that he would not coach Andre anymore. "It's not like it used to be," Bollettieri told the media. "Whether he'll ever reach his greatest potential, no one knows." It turned out that Bollettieri had dumped Andre for Boris Becker. Andre was crushed. He hit rock bottom six weeks later at the U.S. Open when he lost in the opening round to little-known Thomas Enqvist. Andre called the stunning loss "a setback" and went home.

A young tennis player in Las Vegas gets tips from Andre.
He encourages youngsters through the Agassi Foundation.

On Top—Again!

Andre was still heartbroken over the letter from Bollettieri when another letter arrived. This one was sent by fax machine from Africa. The letter was from Brooke Shields.

Brooke was a child model who had become an actor and sex symbol. She had been pushed hard and molded at an early age by strict parents, just as Andre had. Lyndie Benson, the wife of pop saxophonist Kenny G, kept encouraging Brooke to write to Andre. "I just feel you two have the same heart," Benson told Brooke. So Brooke, who was in Africa making a movie, finally sent Andre an introductory note. Andre faxed back a letter. "Then she sent back a novel," Andre says. Soon they were sending faxes back and forth every day. "We couldn't see each other or speak to each other," Brooke remembers, "so it was this strangely private, very personal way of meeting."

Brooke's grandfather was Frank Shields, who had been a U.S. Open finalist in 1930. But that is not what Andre and Brooke had in common. "We've both gone through a lot of the same things," Andre said. "We were both celebrities young, and so we have a similar history together."

After Brooke returned to New York from Africa, they talked on the phone every day for several weeks. In December, three months after the first letter, they met at a Los Angeles restaurant. "We could hardly look at each other, hardly eat our food," Brooke says.

On December 20, Andre had surgery on his wrist. Becoming friends with Brooke had put him in good spirits. He felt he was ready for the operation. He had been undergoing psychotherapy to work out some problems with his father and his upbringing. He was training in the gym with fitness coach Gil Reyes nearly four hours a day, lifting weights and running on the treadmill. He was dieting like never before, eating bagels and coffee for breakfast, a turkey sandwich with mustard for lunch, and pasta for dinner. He still ate candy to satisfy his sweet tooth, but only low-fat kinds like Starbursts, Skittles, and Red Vines. The only thing holding him back from regaining tennis greatness was his wrist.

Richard Scheinberg, the doctor who three years earlier had rebuilt the wrist of Jimmy Connors, performed a 75-minute operation. Scheinberg found more damage in Andre's wrist than anyone had expected, but the surgery was a complete success. "It was about the scariest thing I've ever done," Andre admitted, "but the fear of surgery was actually worse than the surgery itself."

Next, Andre improved the health of his finances. He and Perry Rogers formed Agassi Enterprises. Rogers immediately landed a rich endorsement package for Andre with Nike that would pay him nearly $150 million over 10 years. Then they started the Andre Agassi Foundation through which Andre gives money to help needy youngsters in Las Vegas. Andre bought a house for his parents and one for Reyes.

Andre was ready to begin his comeback. "I'm going to take my career to a place it's never been," he said. In March, he returned to the pro tour in Scottsdale, Arizona, with a two-inch purplish scar on his right wrist. He won the tournament without losing a set.

Despite that strong showing, Andre decided he needed a coach. He and Rogers wrote down a list of possible coaches. Andre took his first choice, Brad Gilbert, to lunch the following week. Gilbert expressed an interest in working with Andre. The next day, they were on the court, trying out different strokes.

Gilbert tinkered with Andre's game, getting him to serve harder, come to the net more, and take the offensive. Andre struggled at first with the changes. But he was patient and trusted Gilbert's ideas.

And then it all came together one day on a practice court in Toronto. "I was working really hard," Andre said, "and suddenly all the shots started to click, and my confidence just picked up." At the Canadian Open, with Brooke watching from the stands, Andre breezed through six opponents to win the title.

At the U.S. Open two weeks later, Andre was unseeded for the first time in seven years. Being unseeded meant that Andre would have a long, tough path to the finals. But Andre wasn't worried.

Andre breezed through the first rounds and then played Michael Chang in the fourth round on the Stadium court. He wore down Chang in five grueling sets. "This is the best I have ever hit the tennis ball, absolutely," Andre said afterward. He continued to use his racket like a power lawn mower in the quarterfinal round by routing tough baseliner Thomas Muster in straight sets. "He has raised his game," Muster observed. In the semifinal round, Agassi trounced hard-serving Todd Martin in four sets.

At 1 o'clock the next morning, on the day of the final against Michael Stich, Andre was on the phone with Gilbert, discussing strategy. The last thing Andre said before he hung up was, "There's no way Stich is leaving here with my title." Wearing black socks and with a ponytail hanging out of his hat, Andre trounced Stich in three straight sets to win the Grand Slam event. The score was 6–1, 7–6, 7–5

His 1994 U.S. Open victory over Michael Stich brought Andre to his knees.

In the final game of the match, Stich hit a wild forehand and netted a backhand and Andre reached championship point. All around the stadium, children were moving down toward the court to be close when Andre won. They wanted to have a chance to catch a shirt when he began throwing them from his bag. With the crowd buzzing and a hint of fall in the air, Andre whacked a topspin forehand that clipped the sideline. Stich barely returned it. Andre belted a backhand half-volley to win. Then he dropped his racket and looked to Gilbert and Brooke. He tried to yell, "I can't believe it," over the roar in the stadium. He sank to his knees and Stich walked around the net and picked him up off the ground. Then Andre ran over and kissed Brooke.

"When I won Wimbledon, it was a relief," Andre said. "Winning this one, I feel I've made a surge forward. There's a difference between saying, 'Whew, I did it,' and saying, 'Yes, I can do it.' "

Andre had started the 1994 season ranked the 34th best male player in the world. He left New York in September saying "I can be the best player in the world." Six months later, he was.

Just before Christmas, Andre decided to do something radical. "I decided," he said, "to cut my hair off." He sat in Brooke's kitchen with a hairstylist from a Manhattan salon holding a pair of scissors over his head. Finally, the stylist lifted the ponytail and cut it off with one stroke. "Oh that feels weird," Andre said.

Three weeks later, Andre took his new look halfway around the world to Melbourne to compete for the first time in the Australian Open. He appeared on the court for the first round with a shaved head, a sharply pointed goatee, two silver hoop earrings the size of thick wedding rings, and a bandanna. He looked like a pirate and, one by one, he made his opponents walk the plank. Andre quickly disposed of Grant Stafford in the first round.

In the second round, a hundred boys and a few girls watched from the stands with freshly shaved heads as Andre rolled to another straight-sets victory. He did so again in the third round. On the eve of the quarterfinals, Andre rented a scary Freddy Krueger movie and watched it with Gilbert and Reyes. Then he blitzed Australian Patrick Rafter in the fourth round. "He made me look silly," said Rafter.

The night before the quarterfinals, Andre's movie choice was *Die Hard*. Then Andre walloped Yevgeny Kafelnikov in straight sets. "No chance, no chance, no chance," Kafelnikov said of his prospects of winning. The night before the semifinals, Andre watched *Die Hard 2: Die Harder.* Then he thumped Aaron Krickstein. "Pretty much impossible," Krickstein said of his chances. On the eve of the final, Andre picked a classic—*The Exorcist*. Then he played a classic final match against hard-working Pete Sampras.

Andre and Pete are good friends but intense rivals. They even made a commercial together in which they climb out of taxicabs in the middle of the street in San Francisco. They set up a tennis court and start going at it. "The excitement between Pete and me is way beyond anything I experience playing the other guys," Andre says. And Sampras agrees. "Andre is the guy who puts tennis on the front page, and to go down in history with him as one of the great rivalries in tennis, that would be the ultimate," said Sampras.

Andre won the Australian Open for his third Grand Slam.

Andre lost the first set to Sampras, 4–6. That was the only set Andre lost in the two-week tournament. He roared back to sweep the next three sets, 6–1, 7–6, 6–4, to beat Sampras and win his third Grand Slam.

While the final was being played, Brooke was in New York, performing in the Broadway play *Grease*. Between each scene and during every costume change, Brooke would come offstage. "What's the score?" she'd call to the crew members, who were watching the match on television.

After Andre finished the victory with an ace, he waved and bowed to the screaming crowd. "I came here believing in myself," he told reporters later. "I've come to terms with myself, and with my tennis. It used to be, I felt I had to live up to something, I had to validate what I did in TV commercials. Now I still have fun with the clothes and the commercials and stuff, but everything has its rightful place."

Andre also has come to terms with his father. Andre has accepted that he was thrust into a world of tennis without a choice. "I missed out on a lot," Andre says, "but I can always talk to my best friend Perry when I want to know what it was like to be a normal teenager." Andre's father understands that he can't interfere anymore in his son's decisions. "What we did was more difficult than hitting the California lottery," Mike says of driving young Andre to be a pro. "The real sacrifice was Andre's childhood."

Andre had hoped to play Sampras again in the 1996 U.S. Open final, but Michael Chang defeated Andre in the semifinals. Still, Andre wasn't discouraged. He was mature enough to realize that he didn't have to win every match to be happy playing tennis.

"People think I've been this preplanned marketing package, but that was never the case," Andre said. "Success just sort of happened to me. Maybe I was rewarded too quickly. For me to be doing commercials and never winning a Grand Slam tournament, that left me with a bad rap—all image, no substance. Well, I've worked hard to be where I am now. Pete Sampras has shown me that hard work and patience pay off. If you do your best and do it long enough, suddenly you'll be there. You'll be No. 1."

Career Highlights

Year	Year-end Ranking	Tournaments Played	Tournaments Won	Matches Won-Lost	Grand Slams Won
1988	3	16	6	63-11	0
1989	7	19	1	41-19	0
1990	4	13	4	44-11	0
1991	10	18	2	38-17	0
1992	9	17	3	42-14	1
1993	24	13	2	33-11	0
1994	2	18	5	51-13	1
1995	2	16	7	73-9	1
1996	7	14	3	38-12	0
Totals	—	144	34	423-117	3

- 1992 – won Wimbledon men's singles title
- 1994 – won U.S. Open men's singles title
- 1995 – won Australian Open men's singles title
- 1996 – won Olympics men's singles title

Glossary

break point: The point with which the player returning serve wins a game.

double fault: A loss of a point because the serving player didn't get either serve attempt in.

held serve: The winning of a game by the player who served.

passing shot: A shot that drives the ball to one side of and past an opponent.

serve-and-volley game: A style of playing in which a player rushes to the net after serving in order to hit the opponent's return before it bounces on the server's side.

straight sets: A match in which one player wins all the sets played. Professional male players play best-of-five matches, which means the first player to win three sets wins the match. If one player wins the first three sets, that player has won in straight sets.

tiebreaker: A 12-point playoff to decide the winner of a set after both players have won six games. One player must win at least seven points and at least two points more than his or her opponent.

Index

ACKNOWLEDGMENTS

Photographs are reproduced with the permission of: pp. 1, 6, © John Klein; p. 2, Archive Photos/Popperfoto; p. 9, Archive Photos/Darlene Hammond; pp. 10, 60, Clive Brunskill/ALLSPORT; p. 11, ArchiveReuters/Kevin Lamarque/Archive Photos; p. 14, Sportschrome East/West Laurie Warner; pp. 19, 22, 46, 48, 49, © Carol L. Newsom; p. 25, Simon Bruty/ALLSPORT; pp. 27, 28, Cynthia Lum; pp. 30, 37, UPI/CORBIS-BETTMANN; pp. 33, 40, 52, REUTERS/BETTMANN; p. 34, Archive/Express Newspapers; p. 38, Rick Stewart/ALLSPORT; p. 45, Bob Martin/ALLSPORT; pp. 51, 57, REUTERS/CORBIS-BETTMANN.

Front cover photograph by Stephen Dunn/ALLSPORT. Back cover photograph by ALLSPORT. Artwork by Michael Tacheny.